Rocky Mountain
Wildflowers
Pocket Guide

by David Dahms

Front Cover:
Blue Columbine (*Aquilegia coerulea*)

Back Cover:
Wood Lily (*Lilium philadelphicum*)
Scarlet Gilia (*Ipomopsis aggregata*)

published by
Paragon Press
991 Ridge West Drive
Windsor, CO 80550

www.paragon-press.com

ISBN 0-9646359-2-5

Printed in South Korea

Ecosystems

	approx elevation in Colorado	approx elevation in Montana
Plains	up to 5,500 ft	up to 3,500 ft
Foothills	5,500 - 6,500 ft	3,500 - 4,000 ft
Montane	6,500 - 9,500 ft	4,000 - 6,500 ft
Subalpine	9,500 - 11,500 ft	6,500 - 7,500 ft
Alpine	11,500 - up	7,500 - up

You would be wise not to randomly eat wild plants. Many plants are mildly toxic while others are highly poisonous. A deadly plant could be tragically mistaken for a safe look-alike relative. A name like "Death Camas" certainly conveys toxicity; yet many seemingly innocuous plants can make you sick too. Please don't arbitrarily taste wild plants or it may be a very unpleasant experience for you or your heirs.

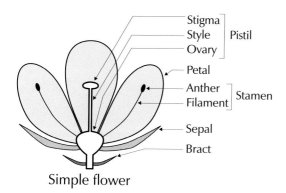

Simple flower

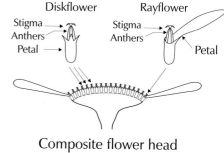

Composite flower head

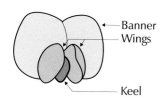

Pea-family flower

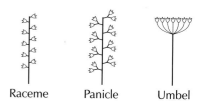

Inflorescence (flower clusters)

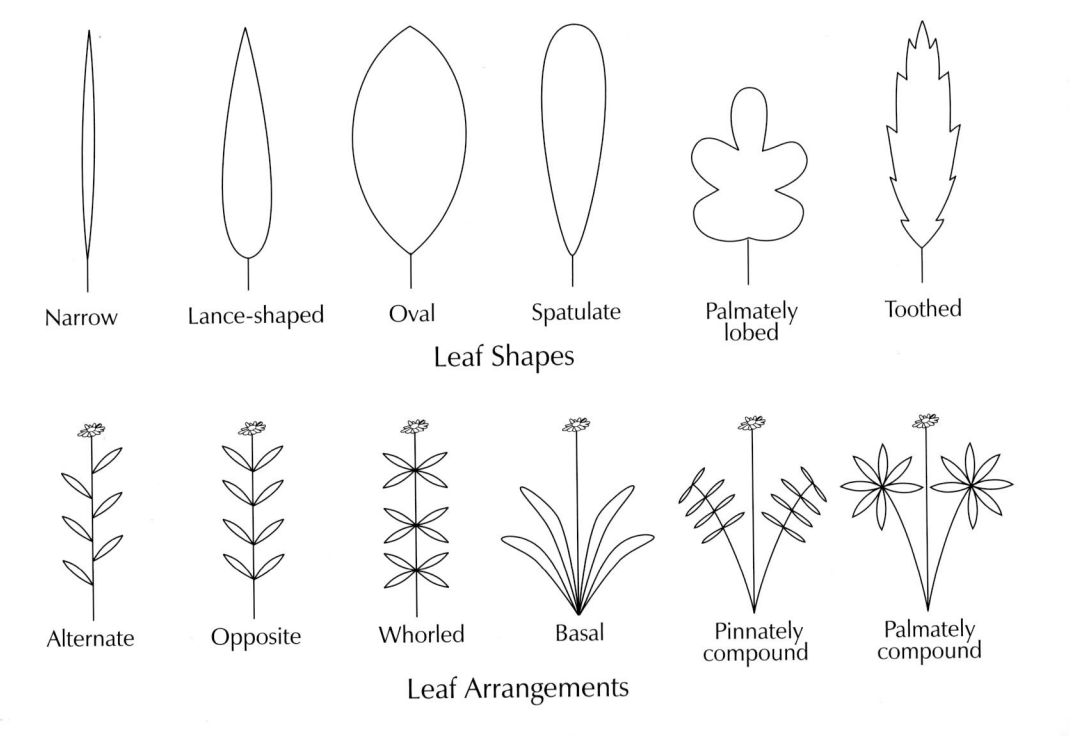

Narrow Lance-shaped Oval Spatulate Palmately lobed Toothed

Leaf Shapes

Alternate Opposite Whorled Basal Pinnately compound Palmately compound

Leaf Arrangements

MOUNTAIN HAREBELL
BELLFLOWER

Campanula rotundifolia
Bellflower family

Flowers: Five lavender-blue petals joined into bell-shaped blossoms, which hang from the top of a tall, thin stem.

Leaves: Thin, alternate leaves along the stem and occasionally a few oval basal leaves.

Size: 4-12 inches; flowers to 1 inch wide.

Season: June to September

Habitat: Foothills to Alpine
Very common in dry open areas, meadows, forest clearings and tundra sites.

PARRY HAREBELL

Campanula parryi
Bellflower family

Flowers: One upward-facing, open bell-shaped blossom with five violet-blue petals.

Leaves: Narrow and alternate.

Size: to 12 inches tall; flowers ½-¾ inch wide.

Season: July and August

Habitat: Montane and Subalpine
Found in moist meadow areas.

LANCELEAF CHIMING BELLS

Mertensia lanceolata
Borage family

Flowers: Narrow, bell-shaped, nodding blossoms hang in dense clusters. Fresh pink buds mature into light blue bells before finally dropping off, leaving the style.

Leaves: Alternate, bluish green, lance-shaped and soft, with a prominent center vein.

Size: to 12 inches tall; flowers ¾-1 inch long.

Season: May to August

Habitat: Foothills to Alpine
Very common in dry open areas.

TALL CHIMING BELLS

Mertensia ciliata
Borage family

Flowers: Light blue petals form the tubular, bell-shaped blossoms, hanging in clusters at the top of the tall stem.

Leaves: Wide lance-shaped leaves alternate along stem.

Size: up to 4 ft; flowers 1 inch long.

Season: June to August

Habitat: Montane to Alpine
Abundant in damp and wet areas, especially along creeks and streams.

ALPINE FORGET-ME-NOT

Eritrichum aretioides
Borage family

Flowers: Small flowers with five bright blue petals and yellow centers, in a dense cluster. Occasionally white.

Leaves: A ground-hugging cushion of tiny, thick, hairy, silvery-green leaves.

Size: 1 inch tall; flowers ¼ inch wide.

Season: June and July

Habitat: Alpine
Prefers dry, rocky areas.

Notes: One of the first tundra flowers to bloom in the summer.

WILD BLUE FLAX

Adenolinum lewisii
Flax family

Flowers: A sky-blue flower with five fragile petals atop a thin, tough stem.

Leaves: Many narrow, linear leaves alternate along the stem.

Size: up to 2 ft; flowers 1 inch wide.

Season: May to August

Habitat: Plains to Subalpine Common in dry sites and roadsides.

Notes: Petals drop off after one morning, but another bud will bloom the next day.

FRINGED GENTIAN

Gentianopsis thermalis
Gentian family

Flowers: A deep-blue or purple upright flower with four fringed petals that spread from the light-colored, tubular throat. Sepals are long, pointed and green.

Leaves: Fairly narrow and opposite, along a stout, straight stem.

Size: 4-16 inches tall; flowers 1-2 inches wide.

Season: July to September

Habitat: Montane and Subalpine Prefers moist areas in full sun. Also found around thermal features in Yellowstone.

MOUNTAIN GENTIAN
PARRY GENTIAN

Pneumonathe parryi
Gentian family

Flowers: Several upright barrel-shaped blue blossoms with light green bases on an erect stem. Five petals and five sepals form the barrel, which spreads into five wide, pointed lobes.

Leaves: Opposite, narrowly oval, smooth.

Size: 6-18 inches; flowers to 1 inch wide.

Season: August and September

Habitat: Montane and Subalpine Prefers open, sunny sites.

Notes: These flowers close rapidly when clouds approach.

BLUE COLUMBINE

Aquilegia coerulea
Hellebore family

Flowers: Five rounded white petals taper into narrow trailing spurs, backed by five large blue pointed sepals, with many contrasting yellow stamens in the center.

Leaves: Mostly basal with rounded lobes.

Size: 1-2 ft tall; flowers 2-4 inches wide.

Season: July to August

Habitat: Foothills to Alpine
Found in moist open areas, aspen groves and rocky slopes.

Notes: This unmistakable beauty is the state flower of Colorado.

13

EARLY LARKSPUR
NELSON LARKSPUR
Delphinium nuttallianum (formerly D. nelsonii)
Hellebore family

Flowers: Deep blue flowers with five showy sepals, one forming a conspicuous rear spur. There are also four small central petals. The upper pair white with blue lines and the lower pair purple, covering a spray of greenish stamens. Flowers are loosely clustered on a smooth stem.

Leaves: Deeply palmately divided into narrow leaflets with a long stem, mostly basal.

Size: 4-12 inches tall; flowers ¾ inch long.

Season: May to June

Habitat: Foothills and Montane Prefers dry open forest areas.

SUBALPINE LARKSPUR

Delphinium barbeyi
Hellebore family

Flowers: Dark navy-blue flowers in a dense cluster atop a tall, strong stem. Flowers have five large, showy sepals, one extending back to form a spur. There are four tiny central petals, the upper pair fringed with white.

Leaves: Large, smooth, palmately divided, with toothed edges.

Size: 3-6 ft; flowers ¾ inch wide.

Season: July and August

Habitat: Subalpine
Grows in clumps in very wet areas, such as stream banks.

15

BLUE-EYED GRASS

Sisyrinchium montanum
Iris family

Flowers: Small deep-blue flowers with yellowish centers, three pointed petals and three identical sepals on a flat stem.

Leaves: Long and very narrow.

Size: 5-20 inches; flowers ½ inch wide.

Season: June to August

Habitat: Plains to Montane
Found in open meadow and grassy areas.

WILD IRIS
BLUE FLAG

Iris missouriensis
Iris family

Flowers: An unmistakable blue-purple flower, with three erect petals and three drooping orange-streaked sepals.

Leaves: Basal, narrow, tough and pointed, nearly as tall as the flower stalk.

Size: 8-20 inches; flowers 2-4 inches wide.

Season: May to July

Habitat: Foothills and Montane
Prefers open meadow areas which are very moist in the spring.

SILVERY LUPINE

Lupinus argenteus
Pea family

Flowers: Light-blue pea-type flowers, clustered along the top of a tall slender stem.

Leaves: Palmately compound with 5-9 narrow, silvery leaflets.

Size: 1-2 ft tall; flowers ½ inch wide.

Season: May to August

Habitat: Foothills to Subalpine Common in meadows, fields and roadsides.

JACOB'S LADDER

Polemonium pulcherrimum delicatum
Phlox family

Flowers: Light bluish-lavender flowers with five pointed petals and five long stamens, in loose clusters on a weak stem.

Leaves: Basal, pinnately compound with many pairs of narrow leaflets, like a ladder.

Size: 5-10 inches; flowers ½ inch wide.

Season: June to August

Habitat: Subalpine
Prefers moist shady forest areas.

Notes: This plant has a slight musky odor.

MONKSHOOD

Aconitum columbianum
Hellebore family

Flowers: Five dark purple sepals form an unusual hood-shaped flower, enclosing the stamens and tiny negligible petals, with an opening near the bottom for entry of pollinating insects. Flowers are loosely arranged near the top of a tall, thin stem.

Leaves: Broad, deeply palmately divided, and toothed.

Size: to 7 ft tall; flowers 1-1½ inches long.

Season: June to August

Habitat: Montane and Subalpine Grows in moist areas, near streams and seeps.

Notes: Creamy light green or white variants are sometimes found.

TANSY ASTER

Machaeranthera bigelovii
Aster family

Flowers: A composite flowerhead with purple rays and a yellow center, and many hook-shaped sticky bracts.

Leaves: Long and linear, with several small teeth. Lower leaves distinctly toothed.

Size: 1-3 ft; flowers 1-1½ inches wide.

Season: August and September

Habitat: Foothills and Montane
Very common in meadows, roadsides and disturbed areas.

PINNATE-LEAVED DAISY

Erigeron pinnatisectus
Aster family

Flowers: Many thin lavender ray flowers around a yellow central disk, with hairy bracts.

Leaves: Basal, to 3 inches long, pinnately dissected into thin lobes.

Size: to 5 inches tall; flowers 1 inch wide.

Season: late June to August

Habitat: Alpine
Grows in high meadows and tundra.

SHOWY DAISY
ASPEN DAISY

Erigeron speciosus
Aster family

Flowers: Composite head with many thin purple rays and yellowish central disks.

Leaves: Many long, smooth, lance-shaped, alternate leaves.

Size: 1-2 ft tall; flowers 1 inch wide.

Season: June to August

Habitat: Foothills to Subalpine Abundant in meadows and forest clearings, often found in aspen groves. This is a very common daisy of the montane zone.

GAYFEATHER
BLAZING STAR

Liatris punctata
Aster family

Flowers: Many tiny purple flowers tightly clustered in a crowded spike, each with long purple extensions protruding from the styles, giving an overall feathery appearance.

Leaves: Linear, with rough edges.

Size: 8-24 inches; flowers ½ inch wide.

Season: August and September

Habitat: Plains to lower Montane Dry open areas, such as gravelly roadsides.

PASQUEFLOWER

Pulsatilla patens multifida
Buttercup family

Flowers: A round cup formed by six hairy, lavender sepals and many bright yellow stamens, nestled in a cluster of furry bracts.

Leaves: A few basal, narrowly divided leaves, which appear after the flower.

Size: to 12 inches tall; flowers 1 inch wide.

Season: March to June

Habitat: Plains to Alpine
Common in many areas, dry plains, hillsides, forest floors, to tundra.

Notes: These are among the first flowers to bloom in the spring. Pasqueflower is the state flower of South Dakota.

SUGARBOWLS
LEATHERFLOWER

Coriflora hirsutissima
Buttercup family

Flowers: Dark purple, hairy, bell-shaped blossoms hang from tough stems. The flowers have four tough, leathery sepals, no petals, and many yellow stamens.

Leaves: Opposite, narrow, finely divided several times, covered with fine hairs.

Size: 1-2 ft; flowers 1 inch long.

Season: May and June

Habitat: Plains and Foothills
Dry open areas, hillsides and fields.

Notes: As the plant matures, the styles become long plumes resulting in a fuzzy white head.

DUSKY PENSTEMON
WHIPPLE PENSTEMON

Penstemon whippleanus
Figwort family

Flowers: Tubular flowers with two-lobed upper lip and and three-lobed lower lip. Usually dark purple or maroon, but sometimes white.

Leaves: Opposite, narrow and pointed, wider near the ground.

Size: 4-18 inches tall; flowers 1½ inch long.

Season: July and August

Habitat: Subalpine and Alpine
Grows in open exposed sites, rocky areas, roadsides and tundra.

Notes: This two-lipped, five-lobed shape is characteristic of all penstemons, and there are many species of them.

27

LOW PENSTEMON
BLUEMIST PENSTEMON

Penstemon virens
Figwort family

Flowers: Blue-violet tubular flowers, each with a two-lobed upper lip and three-lobed lower lip, near the top of an erect, hairy stem.

Leaves: Opposite, bright green, smooth and slightly toothed.

Size: 6-10 inches; flowers ½-¾ inch wide.

Season: May to July

Habitat: Foothills to lower Subalpine Common on dry, rocky hillsides of Colorado and Wyoming.

Notes: "Penstemon" means "five stamens." One is typically larger and extends out of the flower. Because this resembles a tongue, penstemons are nicknamed Beardtongue.

28

ONE-SIDED PENSTEMON
TALL PENSTEMON

Penstemon virgatus asa-grayi
Figwort family

Flowers: Bluish-purple tubular flowers flare into two-lobed upper lip and three-lobed lower lip. Protruding stamen is smooth. Blossoms are clustered along one side of the tall upright stem.

Leaves: Opposite, lance-shaped, smooth.

Size: to 30 inches tall; flowers ¾-1 inch wide.

Season: June to August

Habitat: Foothills and Montane
Very common in dry open areas, roadsides, hillsides and meadows.

Notes: A similar one-sided penstemon, *Penstemon secundiflorus*, has a hairy stamen.

29

WILD GERANIUM

Geranium caespitosum (formerly *G. fremontii*)
Geranium family

Flowers: Five rounded lavender petals with dark vein lines, five sepals, and ten stamens.

Leaves: Deeply cut into 5-7 palmate lobes.

Size: 1-2 ft; flowers ¾-1 inch wide.

Season: May to August

Habitat: Foothills and Montane
Grows in dry meadows, hillsides, fields, forest openings and clearings.

Notes: Related to White Geranium (p 74).

30

SKY PILOT

Polemonium viscosum
Phlox family

Flowers: Blue-violet cone-shaped flowers in tight groups with contrasting orange anthers. Occasionally the flowers are creamy white.

Leaves: Long, narrow, basal leaves, pinnately compound with many tiny oval leaflets.

Size: to 12 inches tall; flowers ¾ inch wide.

Season: late June to August

Habitat: Alpine
Found on rugged tundra slopes, snuggled in cracks between rocks.

Notes: This plant has a strong musky odor, hence the nickname Skunkweed.

HORSEMINT
BEEBALM
WILD BERGAMOT
Monarda fistulosa menthifolia
Mint family

Flowers: A magenta or purple blossom of narrow, tubular flowers radiating from an upward-facing head atop a stout, square stem.

Leaves: Opposite, oval, with small teeth.

Size: 1-2 ft tall; flower heads 1-3 inches wide.

Season: June to August

Habitat: Plains to Montane
Often found in clumps in sunny, dry foothill meadows, fields and roadsides.

Notes: This plant is a magnet for bees and butterflies, but is quite unsavory to horses in spite of its common name.

SKULLCAP

Scutellaria brittonii
Mint family

Flowers: Tubular purple flowers with two lips. The upper lip has a distinctive velvety crest and the large lower lip has white ribs. Flower pairs are located midway along the stem, attached at the same point as leaves.

Leaves: Narrowly oval, opposite leaves.

Size: 4-10 inches; flowers ¾-1 inch long.

Season: May to July

Habitat: Foothills and Montane
Dry open hillsides, woods and grassy areas.

COLORADO LOCO
LAMBERT LOCO

Oxytropis lambertii
Pea family

Flowers: Bright purple or magenta pea-type flowers loosely clustered near the top of a leafless, vertical stalk.

Leaves: Basal, pinnately compound with narrow leaflets.

Size: 4-16 inches tall; flowers to 1 inch wide.

Season: May to August

Habitat: Plains to Montane Commonly found on sunny, dry hillsides, meadows and roadsides.

Notes: Light purple plants may result of hybridization with White Loco (p 86).

PURPLE FRINGE

Phacelia sericea
Waterleaf family

Flowers: Many tiny purple flowers tightly packed along a vertical spike, with conspicuously protruding yellow stamens.

Leaves: Finely divided, silvery and hairy.

Size: 4-12 inches; flowers ¼ inch wide.

Season: June to August

Habitat: Montane to Alpine
Common in dry exposed areas, roadsides, forest clearings, to sheltered tundra areas.

FIREWEED

Chamerion danielsii (formerly *C. angustifolium*)
Evening primrose family

Flowers: Bright reddish-purple flowers with four petals, in a long spire on a tall stem. Only a few flowers bloom at a time, beginning from the bottom of the raceme and progressing upwards.

Leaves: Long, lance-shaped, alternate.

Size: to 6 ft tall; flowers 1 inch wide.

Season: July and August

Habitat: Montane and Subalpine Abundant in open areas, roadsides, disturbed or cleared land.

Notes: Its common name is derived from its ability to rapidly colonize recently burned areas after a forest fire, not its reddish color.

LITTLE PINK ELEPHANTS
ELEPHANT HEAD

Pedicularis groenlandica
Figwort family

Flowers: A dense vertical spike of distinctive magenta flowers which resemble elephants' heads. The upper petal bulges at the top, then tapers and curves upward, resembling an elephant's forehead and trunk. Three other petals form the ears and lower lip.

Leaves: Pinnately lobed, fern-like, red-tinted.

Size: 6-24 inches; flowers ½ inch wide.

Season: late July and August

Habitat: Montane to Alpine
Found in moist and wet marshy meadows, usually occurring in "herds."

SCARLET PAINTBRUSH

Castilleja miniata
Figwort family

Flowers: A cluster of bright red, showy bracts which resembles a brush. Flowers are actually green, very narrow and tubular, and are mostly hidden by the colorful red bracts.

Leaves: Lance-shaped, alternate.

Size: to 2 ft tall; flowers 1 inch long.

Season: June to August

Habitat: Montane and lower Subalpine Common in open meadows and hillsides.

Notes: Another similar red paintbrush is the Rosy Paintbrush (*C. rhexifolia*) which occurs in the subalpine zone.

WYOMING PAINTBRUSH
NARROWLEAF PAINTBRUSH

Castilleja linariifolia
Figwort family

Flowers: The flowers are the long, narrow, green tubes which extend well beyond the brilliant red bracts.

Leaves: Narrow and alternate.

Size: 1-2 ft tall; flowers 1-1½ inches long.

Season: June to September

Habitat: Foothills and Montane
Common in dry open meadows and hillsides, often near sagebrush.

Notes: This is the state flower of Wyoming.

BOG LAUREL
SWAMP LAUREL

Kalmia microphylla
Heath family

Flowers: Dainty pink flowers with five united petals in an open bowl shape. Flowers usually occur in groups of 2-10, each with a red stem, on an evergreen, prostrate shrub.

Leaves: Lance-shaped, opposite and smooth, green on top and gray below.

Size: 6-12 inches tall; flowers ½-¾ inch wide.

Season: July and August

Habitat: Subalpine
Grows in very wet areas, such as lakeshores, marshes and seeps.

RED COLUMBINE

Aquilegia elegantula
Hellebore family

Flowers: Very distinctive nodding flowers with five red petals that extend rearward as long spurs. Five red and yellow sepals surround a spray of yellow stamens.

Leaves: Mostly basal with rounded lobes.

Size: 1-2 ft tall; flowers 1-2 inches long.

Season: June to August

Habitat: Montane and Subalpine Grows in moist meadows and open woods, primarily on the Western Slope.

WOOD LILY

Lilium philadelphicum
Lily family

Flowers: Six large, curved, orange-red tepals with dark spots on their bases and obvious dark purple anthers. This spectacular flower faces upward on a stout, vertical stem.

Leaves: Lance-shaped, in whorls.

Size: to 2 ft; flowers to 3 inches wide.

Season: Late June and July

Habitat: Foothills and Montane Occasionally found in moist meadows and open woods. This magnificent flower is very rare and should never be picked.

Notes: When petals and sepals look identical, they are all called "tepals."

GEYER ONION

Allium geyeri
Onion family

Flowers: An upright umbel of small pink flowers, each with six tepals. A white papery bract surrounds the base of the umbel.

Leaves: Three very narrow, long, basal leaves.

Size: to 12 inches tall; flowers ¼ inch tall.

Season: June to August

Habitat: Foothills to Alpine
Grows in moist meadows and open forests.

NODDING ONION

Allium cernuum
Onion family

Flowers: A cluster of small, light-pink, round blossoms with six tiny tepals and protruding stamens. Each flower hangs from the end of the arched main stem on a thin stalk, like a starburst.

Leaves: Basal, long, narrow and smooth.

Size: to 12 inches tall; flowers ¼ inch wide.

Season: June to September

Habitat: Foothills to Subalpine
Common in slightly moist forest clearings, fields and open meadows.

44

CALYPSO ORCHID
FAIRY SLIPPER

Calypso bulbosa
Orchid family

Flowers: One enlarged petal forms the scoop-shaped slipper, adorned with purple stripes and yellow hairs. Two other petals and three sepals, all narrow and bright magenta, rise behind the slipper.

Leaves: One broadly oval, basal leaf.

Size: to 8 inches; flowers 1-1½ inch long.

Season: May and June

Habitat: Montane and Subalpine
Shady forest areas with a layer of duff.

Notes: Like many orchids, it depends on a symbiotic relationship with a soil-borne fungus. You should consider yourself very lucky if you see this spectacular flower.

45

SPOTTED CORALROOT

Corallorhiza maculata
Orchid family

Flowers: Three dark reddish-brown sepals and two upper petals spread over the enlarged third petal, which is white with purple spots. Flowers are distributed along the top half of a dark red stem.

Leaves: None

Size: to 20 inches; flowers ½-¾ inch wide.

Season: June and July

Habitat: Montane
Shady forests and woods.

Notes: This plant is a saprophyte, which means it has no chlorophyll to make its own food and instead depends on a fungus in decaying organic material.

46

SCARLET GILIA
FAIRY TRUMPET

Ipomopsis aggregata
Phlox family

Flowers: A brilliant red, trumpet-shaped flower with a long tubular throat that flares into five pointed lobes. Flowers are near the top of long thin stem, mostly on one side.

Leaves: Alternate, pinnately divided, mostly near the ground.

Size: 1-3 ft; flowers 1-2 inches long.

Season: July to September

Habitat: Foothills and Montane Common in open dry areas and roadsides.

Notes: This species may hybridize with White Fairy Trumpet to produce shades of pink. Hummingbirds love these flowers.

PINEDROPS

Pterospora andromedea
Pinesap family

Flowers: Many small, red and white, bell-shaped flowers, each on its own short stalk, hang from the main unbranched red stem.

Leaves: Short, narrow, scaly bracts.

Size: 1-3 ft; flowers ¼-½ inch long.

Season: June to August

Habitat: Montane
Grows in the pine needle duff and organic debris on forest floors.

Notes: This plant is not green because it is a saprophyte, which means it uses decaying organic material rather than produce its own food by photosynthesis.

MOSS CAMPION

Silene acaulis subacaulescens
Pink family

Flowers: Small pink flowers with five petals in a dense cushion.

Leaves: Basal, small, grass-like.

Size: 1 inch; flowers ¼-½ inch wide.

Season: June to August

Habitat: Alpine
Common in rocky areas on tundra.

FAIRY PRIMROSE

Primula angustifolia
Primrose family

Flowers: Five reddish-purple petals with notched tips, and a yellow center.

Leaves: Short, narrow, and fleshy.

Size: 1-3 inches; flowers ½-¾ inch wide.

Season: June and early July

Habitat: Subalpine and Alpine
Grows in open, dry, rocky areas.

PARRY PRIMROSE

Primula parryi
Primrose family

Flowers: Striking five-petaled flowers, vivid magenta-red with yellow centers, loosely clustered at the top of a stout, smooth stem.

Leaves: Basal, thick, wider near the tips, often taller than the flower stalk.

Size: to 16 inches; flowers 1 inch wide.

Season: July and early August

Habitat: Subalpine and Alpine
Locally abundant in wet marshy areas, and along stream banks and pond shores.

Notes: This plant has a distinct skunky odor.

SHOOTING STAR

Dodecatheon pulchellum
Primrose family

Flowers: Distinctive flowers with four or five bright magenta petals that flare rearward, resembling the tail of a shooting star. Stamens are fused into a dark snout. Several flowers hang from the top of a straight, leafless stalk.

Leaves: Roundish leaves in a basal rosette.

Size: to 16 inches; flowers 1-1½ inches long.

Season: May to July

Habitat: Foothills to Subalpine
Grows in moist areas, near streams and seeps.

52

WILD ROSE

Rosa woodsii
Rose family

Flowers: A large flower, open and showy, with five delicate pink petals and many yellow stamens and pistils in the center.

Leaves: Pinnately compound, with toothed edges. This plant is a shrub with prickly, branched stems.

Size: 1- 6 ft; flowers 1-2½ inches wide.

Season: June to August

Habitat: Plains to Subalpine
Commonly found in open dry areas, hillsides, fields, roadsides and meadows.

KING'S CROWN

Rhodiola integrifolia
Stonecrop family

Flowers: Many tiny, deep-red flowers in a tight cluster atop a stout, fleshy stem.

Leaves: Short, alternate, broadly lance-shaped, equally spaced along the stem.

Size: 4-12 inches; flower head to 1 inch wide.

Season: June to August

Habitat: Subalpine and Alpine
Well-drained rocky and gravelly areas.

QUEEN'S CROWN
ROSE CROWN

Clementsia rhodantha
Stonecrop family

Flowers: A crowded round cluster of many small, five-petaled pink and white flowers on top of a straight, strong stem.

Leaves: Narrow, smooth, fleshy, alternate leaves, all around the stem.

Size: 3-12 inches; flower head to 1 inch wide.

Season: June to August

Habitat: Subalpine and Alpine
Found in moist places, near seeps, streams and ponds.

PINK PYROLA
SWAMP PYROLA

Pyrola rotundifolia asarifolia
Wintergreen family

Flowers: Small round flowers with five petals, light pink to red, hanging near the top of a straight, leafless stalk.

Leaves: Oval, shiny and basal with long stems.

Size: 8-16 inches; flowers ¼ inch wide.

Season: June to August

Habitat: Montane and Subalpine
Grows in shady, moist areas on forest floors.

PORTER ASTER

Aster porteri
Aster family

Flowers: Small composite flower with white rays and a yellow center, on a multiply-branched wiry stem. Yellow centers slowly turn brown with age.

Leaves: Narrow, smooth, alternate.

Size: 8-16 inches; flowers ½-¾ inch wide.

Season: August and September

Habitat: Foothills and Montane Abundant in open, sunny, dry meadows, slopes and roadsides of the central and southern Rockies.

Notes: Asters generally bloom later in the summer than daisies, the rays of asters are generally wider than those of daisies, and bracts of asters appear disorganized.

BLACK-HEADED DAISY

Erigeron melanocephalus
Aster family

Flowers: A single composite flower with white rays around a yellow center. Underside of the flower is covered with many dark woolly hairs.

Leaves: Mostly basal and oval, with a few small leaves along the stem.

Size: 2-6 inches; flowers 1-1½ inches wide.

Season: July to September

Habitat: Subalpine and Alpine
Fairly common in tundra and high forested areas, often near melting snow.

TRAILING DAISY
WHIPLASH DAISY

Erigeron flagellaris
Aster family

Flowers: Small composite flowers with yellow centers and very numerous thin rays that are white on top and pinkish below.

Leaves: Basal, lance-shaped, wider at the tip.

Size: 4-12 inches; flowers ½-¾ inch wide.

Season: May to July

Habitat: Plains to Montane
Common in open, sunny sites, such as meadows and roadsides.

Notes: After blooming profusely early in the summer, this plant forms numerous runners that spread along the ground and start new plants.

PEARLY EVERLASTING

Anaphalis margaritacea
Aster family

Flowers: Small white flowers with pearly white bracts and no rays, in tight clusters.

Leaves: Alternate, narrow, green on top and covered with fine white hairs below.

Size: 12-24 inches; flowers ¼-½ inch wide.

Season: Late July to September

Habitat: Montane and Subalpine Common in disturbed areas, forest clearings, and along roadsides, usually in clumps.

Notes: Its name is due to its longevity in cut flower arrangements.

PUSSYTOES

Antennaria pulcherrima anaphaloides
Aster family

Flowers: Tiny flower heads with papery white bracts in a very dense cluster. These are actually composite flowers with only disc flowers and no ray flowers.

Leaves: Narrow, hairy on both sides, alternate.

Size: 6-12 inches; flowers ¼-½ inch wide.

Season: June to August

Habitat: Foothills to Subalpine
Common in open, sunny meadows and open wooded areas.

Notes: If you rub your fingers on this flower it feels like a cat's paw. There are many other similar species of pussytoes in the area.

SHOWY TOWNSENDIA

Townsendia grandiflora
Aster family

Flowers: A large composite flower with an olive-green center, white rays with purplish undersides, and rows of bristly bracts. There is only one flower on each stem, which is reddish and hairy.

Leaves: Alternate, narrow, and thick.

Size: 2-8 inches; flowers 1-2 inches wide.

Season: May to July

Habitat: Foothills
Grows in sunny, open, dry areas.

Notes: This plant is related to the Easter Daisy *(Townsendia Hookeri)* which blooms very early in the spring.

WILD CHAMOMILE

Matricaria perforata
Aster family

Flowers: Medium-sized composite flowerheads with white rays and bulging yellow centers.

Leaves: Alternate and finely divided into very thin segments.

Size: 8-24 inches; flowers 1-2 inches wide.

Season: July to September

Habitat: Montane and Subalpine
Grows profusely in disturbed areas and along roadsides, mainly on the Western Slope.

Notes: In some areas, this is considered an invasive weed.

YARROW

Achillea lanulosa
Aster family

Flowers: Many tiny flowers with five white rays and yellow disks, clustered in a dense flat-topped umbel on a thin stem.

Leaves: Narrow, long, pinnately dissected into thin leaflets, resembling a feather.

Size: 6-18 inches; flowers ¼-½ inch wide.

Season: June through September

Habitat: Plains to Alpine
Very common in dry open areas, hillsides, roadsides and forest clearings.

Notes: An umbel is a flower cluster much like an umbrella, where all the individual flower stems radiate from one point at the top of the main stem.

64

MINER'S CANDLE

Oreocarya virgata
Borage family

Flowers: Numerous small, five-petaled, white flowers spread along a tall, hairy, strong stem.

Leaves: Narrow, tough and prickly, standing perpendicular to the stem.

Size: 10-24 inches; flowers ½ inch wide.

Season: May to July

Habitat: Foothills and Montane
Grows in gravelly dry sites, such as hillsides, fields and meadows.

BISTORT

Bistorta bistortoides
Buckwheat family

Flowers: A very dense cylindrical cluster of minute flowers with five white sepals and protruding stamens, on a tall, thin stem.

Leaves: Long, narrow, mostly basal.

Size: 8-24 inches; cluster ½-1 inch wide.

Season: June to August

Habitat: Subalpine and Alpine
Very common in high meadows and moist tundra areas.

MOUSE-EAR CHICKWEED

Cerastium strictum
Chickweed family

Flowers: Small white flowers with five petals and greenish-yellow stamens. Petal tips are deeply notched into two round lobes.

Leaves: Narrow, opposite, fuzzy.

Size: 4-12 inches; flowers ½ inch wide.

Season: May to July

Habitat: Plains to Alpine
Very common in dry areas, meadows and forest clearings, sometimes in large patches.

Notes: The two round lobes of a petal resemble a mouse's ears.

SANDWORT
FENDLER SANDWORT

Eremogone fendleri
Chickweed family

Flowers: Small white flowers with five petals. The dark purple spots are the anthers, which eventually fall off.

Leaves: Narrow, rigid and thin, like grass.

Size: 3-10 inches; flowers ¼-½ inch wide.

Season: July and August

Habitat: Foothills to Subalpine
Found in sunny dry locations, hillsides and open forest areas.

68

ALPINE SANDWORT
SANDYWINKS

Lidia obtusiloba
Chickweed family

Flowers: Many small white flowers in a dense cushion, each with five notched petals.

Leaves: Very small, moss-like.

Size: 1-2 inches; flowers ¼-½ inch wide.

Season: July and August

Habitat: Alpine
Common in sandy and rocky dry areas on the tundra, sometimes forming large carpets.

CUTLEAF EVENING PRIMROSE

Oenothera coronopifolia
Evening primrose family

Flowers: Large white flowers with four thin petals and long yellow stamens. Petals quickly turn pink with age.

Leaves: Pinnately cut into thin sections.

Size: 3-12 inches; flowers ¾-1½ inches wide.

Season: June to August

Habitat: Plains to Montane
Common in disturbed areas and roadsides.

Notes: Other white evening primroses of the area include the Nuttall Evening Primrose *(O. nuttalli)* which is taller and has undivided narrow leaves, and the Stemless Evening Primrose *(O. caespitosa)* which is short with larger flowers.

70

DEATH CAMAS

Anticlea elegans
False Hellebore family

Flowers: A star-shaped blossom formed by six pointed creamy-white tepals, each with a green spot at its base. Flowers are loosely distributed near the top of the stem.

Leaves: Long, linear, basal, sparse.

Size: 8-18 inches; flowers ½-¾ inches wide.

Season: June to August

Habitat: Foothills to Alpine
Moist sites in meadows and open woods.

Notes: As you might guess from its name, this plant is very poisonous.

SICKLETOP LOUSEWORT
PARROT'S BEAK

Pedicularis racemosa alba
Figwort family

Flowers: White flowers with two lips, clustered near the top of a reddish stem. Upper lip narrows and curves down and back over the broad, three-lobed lower lip.

Leaves: Simple, lance-shaped, faintly toothed, often with a copper tint.

Size: 8-24 inches; flowers ½-¾ inches wide.

Season: July and August

Habitat: Upper Montane and Subalpine Common in forested areas.

GREEN GENTIAN
MONUMENT PLANT

Frasera speciosa
Gentian family

Flowers: Numerous intricate flowers cover the tall, erect stem. Each flower has four greenish-white petals with purple specks, backed by four pointed sepals. Four curved stamens surround a prominent central ovary.

Leaves: Long and narrow, in whorls.

Size: 2-7 feet tall; flowers ¾-1 inch wide.

Season: July and August

Habitat: Foothills to Subalpine
Open meadows and forest clearings.

Notes: This plant lives many years without blooming as a flat rosette of leaves. In its last year, it sends up its main stem and blooms.

WHITE GERANIUM
RICHARDSON'S GERANIUM

Geranium richardsonii
Geranium family

Flowers: Five white, rounded petals with pink vein lines. Flowers usually in pairs on a tall, thin, branched stem.

Leaves: Palmately cleft into 5-7 pointed lobes, on long stalks.

Size: 1-3 ft; flowers 1 inch wide.

Season: May to August

Habitat: Foothills to Subalpine Commonly found in moist shady areas, woods and forested areas.

Notes: related to Wild Geranium (page 30).

74

GLOBEFLOWER

Trollius albiflorus
Hellebore family

Flowers: Five ivory sepals form a saucer-shaped flower with many yellow stamens and a few central green pistils.

Leaves: Deeply palmately divided into 5-7 lobes with many teeth.

Size: 10-18 inches; flowers 1-1½ inches wide.

Season: June to August

Habitat: Subalpine and Alpine
Locally abundant in moist meadows and marshy areas, usually in clumps.

MARSH MARIGOLD

Psychrophila leptosepala
Hellebore family

Flowers: An open bowl-shaped flower formed by 5-15 narrow oval sepals, mostly white with blue-tinged undersides. Many stamens and pistils form the yellow center.

Leaves: Basal, oval, with a heart-shaped base.

Size: 4-8 inches; flowers 1-1½ inches wide.

Season: June to August

Habitat: Subalpine and Alpine
Locally abundant in wet sites, marshy meadows, and soggy areas near melting snowbanks, early in the alpine summer season. It will grow in standing water.

SAND LILY
STAR LILY

Leucocrinum montanum
Lily family

Flowers: Six white tepals spread widely from a tubular throat. The flowers rise from the center of a clump of leaves, without a stem.

Leaves: Basal, long, linear and folded.

Size: to 8 inches; flower 1 inch wide.

Season: April to June

Habitat: Plains and Foothills
Grows on dry prairies, grassy meadows, open fields and hillsides.

NORTHERN BEDSTRAW

Galium septentrionale
Madder family

Flowers: Numerous tiny white flowers in several dense clusters on a straight stem. Flowers have four pointed, white petals.

Leaves: Narrow, in whorls of four along the square stem.

Size: 8-30 inches; flowers $1/8$ inch wide.

Season: June to August

Habitat: Foothills to Subalpine
Very common on dry areas, roadsides, and open forests.

Notes: Settlers used this plant for mattress stuffing because it retained its loft better than conventional straw.

78

WHITE CHECKERMALLOW
MODEST MALLOW

Sidalcea candida
Mallow family

Flowers: Delicate open white flowers with five thin petals, clustered at the top of an unbranched erect stem. The united stamens form a long tube around the style and spread near the tip, resembling a fountain spray of purple dots.

Leaves: Basal leaves are palmately seven-lobed and toothed. Upper leaves palmately dissected into narrow segments.

Size: 1-3 ft; flowers ¾-1 inch wide.

Season: July and August

Habitat: Montane and Subalpine Grows in moist sites, meadows, aspen groves and streambanks.

SEGO LILY
MARIPOSA LILY

Calochortus gunnisonii
Mariposa family

Flowers: An open cup-shaped flower with three broad white petals, three narrow green sepals, and six conspicuous stamens. The petals have dense brown-yellow hairs near their bases.

Leaves: Long and narrow.

Size: 8-20 inches; flowers 1-2 inches wide.

Season: May through August

Habitat: Foothills and Montane
Common in aspen groves, open meadows, fields and hillsides.

FALSE SOLOMON SEAL
CLASPLEAF SOLOMON PLUME

Maianthemum amplexicaule
Mayflower family

Flowers: Small white flowers in a panicle (branched cluster) on a tall smooth stem. Flowers have three tiny petals and three sepals.

Leaves: Large, broad, pointed, alternate, clasping the stem.

Size: 1-3 ft; flowers $1/8$ inch wide.

Season: May to July

Habitat: Plains to Montane
Grows in moist, shady, wooded areas.

Notes: A similar plant, Star Solomon Plume *(M. stellatum)*, has its six-pointed flowers in an unbranched cluster.

BITTER CRESS
BROOK CRESS

Cardamine cordifolia
Mustard family

Flowers: Bright white four-petaled flowers in a rounded cluster on a leafy stem.

Leaves: Heart-shaped and slightly toothed, with prominent vein lines.

Size: 1-2 ft; flowers ½-¾ inches wide.

Season: June to August

Habitat: Montane and Subalpine Common in very wet sites such as creek and stream banks.

GIANT ANGELICA

Angelica ampla
Parsley family

Flowers: Large round umbels composed of numerous small round umbels of tiny white flowers atop a stout, branched, purple stem.

Leaves: Pinnately compound with large, toothed leaflets.

Size: to 6 ft; flower umbels 4-8 inches wide.

Season: July and August

Habitat: Montane and Subalpine
Grows in very wet areas such as streambanks and lake shores.

COW PARSNIP

Heracleum sphondylium montanum
Parsley family

Flowers: Huge flat-topped umbels of tiny white flowers on a tall, sturdy stem.

Leaves: Very large leaves divided into three toothed lobes.

Size: 4-8 ft; flower umbel 6-12 inches wide.

Season: June to August

Habitat: Foothills and Montane
Abundant in moist and marshy sites, damp forested areas and streambanks.

Notes: An umbel is a flower cluster much like an umbrella, where all the individual flower stems radiate from one point at the top of the main stem.

PORTER LOVAGE
OSHA

Ligusticum porteri
Parsley family

Flowers: Tiny white flowers in small flat-topped umbels which are clustered into large round umbels.

Leaves: Large and finely dissected like a fern.

Size: to 5 ft; flowers ¼ inch wide.

Season: July and August

Habitat: Montane
Grows in open meadows and wooded areas.

ROCKY MOUNTAIN LOCO
WHITE LOCO

Oxytropis sericea
Pea family

Flowers: Numerous white pea-type flowers in a dense tall cluster.

Leaves: Pinnately compound with silvery hairs.

Size: 10-18 inches; flowers ½-¾ inch wide.

Season: June and July

Habitat: Plains to Montane
Grows in dry areas, gravelly slopes and open fields, usually in large colonies.

Notes: This plant may hybridize with Lambert Loco (p34) and produce shades of purple and pink. Sometimes called "Locoweed," its slight toxicity may cause strange behavior in animals that eat it.

86

ALPINE PHLOX

Phlox sibirica pulvinata
Phlox family

Flowers: Numerous small, bluish-tinted white flowers with five rounded petals.

Leaves: Many short, mosslike leaves form a dense ground-hugging cushion.

Size: ½-1 inch; flowers ¼-½ inch wide.

Season: June to August

Habitat: Alpine
Grows in rocky tundra areas.

ALPINE SPRINGBEAUTY
BIG-ROOTED SPRINGBEAUTY

Claytonia megarhiza
Purslane family

Flowers: Five white petals with red veins and two green sepals, arranged around the outside of a round leaf cluster.

Leaves: Fleshy rounded leaves in a flat rosette.

Size: 3-5 inches; flowers ½-¾ inches wide.

Season: July and August

Habitat: Alpine
Grows in rocky tundra areas, often in sheltered crevices between rocks.

CHOKECHERRY

Padus virginiana
Rose family

Flowers: Tiny creamy-white flowers arranged in cylindrical clusters. Flowers mature into dark red or black cherries.

Leaves: Oval with finely toothed edges.

Size: 5-20 ft; flower cluster 1-2 inches wide and about 6 inches long.

Season: May and June

Habitat: Plains to Montane
Very common in moist areas, gulches, ravines, and along roadsides. This plant is a woody shrub that can grow quite large and form thickets. The cherries are an important food for wildlife.

MOUNTAIN DRYAD
WHITE MOUNTAIN AVENS

Dryas octopetala hookeriana
Rose family

Flowers: Creamy-white flowers with eight oval petals and eight sepals, with many yellow stamens in the center.

Leaves: Thick and fleshy, with lobed edges and an embossed surface, in a thick cushion.

Size: 3-8 inches; flowers 1-1½ inch wide.

Season: July and August

Habitat: Alpine
Grows in gravelly tundra sites.

Notes: This plant is actually a dwarf shrub. The styles become fuzzy plumes as the flowers mature.

BOULDER RASPBERRY

Oreobatus deliciosus
Rose family

Flowers: Large white flowers with five thin petals and central cluster of yellow stamens.

Leaves: Generally oval with faint lobes, prominent veins and finely toothed edges. Stems are not prickly.

Size: about 5 ft; flowers 2-3 inches wide.

Season: May and June

Habitat: Plains to Montane
This shrub grows abundantly in sunny open areas, rocky hillsides and roadsides of the eastern slope in Colorado.

Notes: Its fruit is tasteless, not *deliciosus*.

WILD STRAWBERRY

Fragaria virginiana glauca
Rose family

Flowers: White flowers with five petals and five sepals, which will mature into a tiny red berry.

Leaves: Palmately divided into three leaflets with toothed edges.

Size: 2-4 inches; flowers ¾-1 inch wide.

Season: June to August

Habitat: Foothills to Subalpine Common in moist open meadows and forest clearings.

Notes: This plant propagates by sending out ground runners which take root and start new plants.

SNOWBALL SAXIFRAGE

Micranthes rhomboidea
Saxifrage family

Flowers: Tiny conical white flowers with five petals and five sepals, in a round cluster on a tall, leafless stalk.

Leaves: A flat rosette of short-stemmed toothed leaves.

Size: 3-12 inches; flower cluster ½-1 inch wide.

Season: May to August

Habitat: Foothills to Alpine
Grows in open meadows and rocky areas, particularly disturbed sites.

CANADA VIOLET

Viola scopulorum
Violet family

Flowers: Five oval white petals with a yellow throat and purple vein lines. The lower petal has a spur at its tip.

Leaves: Heart-shaped leaves with faint teeth and short stalks along the main stem.

Size: 6-12 inches; flowers ½-¾ inch wide.

Season: May to July

Habitat: Foothills and Montane Grows in moist, shady, wooded areas.

WOOLY ACTINELLA

Tetraneuris brevifolia
Aster family

Flowers: Bright yellow composite flower head. Each has about a dozen stubby rays with three teeth on their tips.

Leaves: Basal, simple, silvery and hairy.

Size: 2-5 inches; flower ¾-1¼ inches wide.

Season: June to August

Habitat: Alpine
Grows in rocky areas of the tundra.

Notes: This flower resembles Rydbergia (p105), but can be distinguished by its small, simple leaves.

HEARTLEAF ARNICA

Arnica cordifolia
Aster family

Flowers: A bright yellow composite flower head on a single hairy stem. There are about ten petal-like rays with notched tips.

Leaves: Two to four pairs of opposite, heart-shaped leaves with faint teeth.

Size: 6-20 inches; flowers 1-2½ inches wide.

Season: June to August

Habitat: Montane and Subalpine
Very common in moist forest areas.

BLACK-EYED SUSAN

Rudbeckia hirta
Aster family

Flowers: Large composite flowerhead with pointed, bright yellow rays and a dark, bulging central disk.

Leaves: Simple, alternate, hairy, long and narrow, along a hairy stem.

Size: 12-20 inches; flower 2-3 inches wide.

Season: June to August

Habitat: Foothills and Montane
Widespread and abundant in open meadows and forest clearings.

TALL CONEFLOWER
CUTLEAF CONEFLOWER
GOLDENGLOW

Rudbeckia ampla
Aster family

Flowers: Large upward-facing flower head with yellow drooping rays and a greenish-brown conical central disk.

Leaves: Palmately lobed, smooth, alternate.

Size: to 6 ft; flowers 2-5 inches wide.

Season: June to August

Habitat: Foothills and Montane Common in moist meadows, open woods and streambanks.

GAILLARDIA
BLANKETFLOWER

Gaillardia aristata
Aster family

Flowers: Large composite flowerhead with many bright yellow rays around a reddish-brown central disk. Rays are often red-tinted at the base.

Leaves: Lance-shaped and hairy.

Size: 10-24 inches; flower 2-3 inches wide.

Season: June to August

Habitat: Plains to Montane
Often found in sunny dry areas, such as meadows and hillsides.

MOUNTAIN GUMWEED

Grindelia subalpina
Aster family

Flowers: Yellow composite flowers with thin, spaced rays and many short, curved bracts. Flower buds are covered with sticky white sap.

Leaves: Alternate, thick, sharply toothed, on a multiply-branched stem.

Size: 8-18 inches; flowers 1-1½ inches wide.

Season: July to September

Habitat: Foothills and Montane
Very common in open meadows, disturbed sites and roadsides.

Notes: A very similar species (*G. squarosa*) appears on the plains and foothills.

YELLOW SALSIFY

Tragopogon dubius major
Aster family

Flowers: Yellow flower heads are composed of ray flowers only. Outer rays are long, and inner ones are short with brown styles. Long green bracts extend beyond the outer rays. Flower matures into a round white seed head like a huge dandelion.

Leaves: Long and thin, like grass, clasping the stem.

Size: 1-4 ft; flower 1-2 inches wide.

Season: May to July

Habitat: Plains and Foothills
Found in open fields, waste places, vacant lots, ditches and roadsides.

ARROWLEAF SENECIO
ARROWLEAF RAGWORT

Senecio triangularis
Aster family

Flowers: Loose clusters of yellow composite flowers on a tall, stout stem. The ray flowers are scattered and appear disorganized.

Leaves: Large, alternate, triangular and coarsely toothed.

Size: 2-5 ft; flowers 1 inch wide.

Season: July to September

Habitat: Subalpine
Grows abundantly in very wet sites such as streambanks.

BLACK-TIPPED SENECIO

Senecio atratus
Aster family

Flowers: Clusters of numerous small yellow composite flowers on a branched stem. The ray flowers are irregularly spaced and curve downward. Bracts have conspicuous black tips.

Leaves: Large, broadly lance-shaped, alternate, weakly toothed, somewhat fleshy, gray-green.

Size: 1-2 ft; flowers ½ inch wide.

Season: July to September

Habitat: Subalpine
Common along road shoulders and gravelly areas.

ORANGE SNEEZEWEED

Dugaldi hoopesii
Aster family

Flowers: Large yellow-orange flowerheads with raised central disks and drooping rays.

Leaves: Alternate, broadly lance-shaped.

Size: 1-4 ft; flower 1-3 inches wide.

Season: July to September

Habitat: Montane
Grows in open fields, meadows, wooded areas and roadsides, mainly west of the Continental Divide.

104

ALPINE SUNFLOWER
RYDBERGIA
OLD MAN OF THE MOUNTAIN

Rydbergia grandiflora
Aster family

Flowers: A single large, yellow composite flower on a hairy short stem. The crowded yellow rays have three tiny lobes at their tips.

Leaves: Mostly basal, divided into many thin segments, and covered with hair.

Size: 2-6 inches; flowers 2-4 inches wide.

Season: July and August

Habitat: Alpine
Conspicuously abundant on high meadows, slopes and ridges of the tundra.

Notes: The head always faces east, away from the prevailing wind. This plant grows for several years before blooming.

105

ASPEN SUNFLOWER

Helianthella quinquenervis
Aster family

Flowers: A large yellow composite flower with 10-20 rays. Flower hangs from the top of a tall straight stem, usually facing east.

Leaves: Large, broadly lance-shaped, opposite and shiny, with five prominent vein lines.

Size: 1-4 ft; flowers 3-4 inches wide.

Season: July and August

Habitat: Montane and Subalpine Primarily moist areas of aspen forests.

DWARF SUNFLOWER
BUSH SUNFLOWER

Helianthus pumilus
Aster family

Flowers: Several large, showy composite flowers on a bushy, branched stem. They have bright yellow rays and brownish-yellow disks.

Leaves: Broadly lance-shaped, opposite with short stalks and very rough like sandpaper.

Size: 1-2 ft; flowers 1-3 inches wide.

Season: July to September

Habitat: Foothills and mid Montane Grows abundantly in open dry areas, hillsides and roadsides, primarily on the eastern slope of Colorado and Wyoming.

SULPHUR FLOWER

Eriogonum umbellatum
Buckwheat family

Flowers: Tiny yellow flowers in dense spherical clusters, 1-2 inches wide. Groups of clusters are attached to the top of main stem by individual short stalks.

Leaves: Oval, wooly underneath.

Size: 4-12 inches; flowers ¼ inch long.

Season: June to August

Habitat: Foothills and Montane Common in dry sites, rocky areas and roadsides.

SNOW BUTTERCUP

Ranunculus adoneus
Buttercup family

Flowers: Cup-shaped flowers with five bright yellow, shiny petals.

Leaves: Divided into many thin segments.

Size: 4-10 inches; flowers ¾-1½ inches wide.

Season: June and July

Habitat: Upper Subalpine and Alpine Common in very wet areas on the tundra. Often found near melting snowbanks or pushing up through the edge of the snow, early in the summer.

COMMON EVENING PRIMROSE

Oenothera villosa
Evening primrose family

Flowers: Bright yellow flowers with four petals and conspicuous stamens on a tall erect stem. Blossoms open in the evening, then turn orange and wither the next day, eventually leaving tubular seed pods.

Leaves: Alternate, lance-shaped, gray-green, hairy, slightly toothed.

Size: 1-3 ft; flowers ¾-1 inch wide.

Season: July to September

Habitat: Plains and Foothills
Grows in open or disturbed areas, such as ditches, fields and roadsides.

BUTTER-AND-EGGS TOADFLAX

Linaria vulgaris
Figwort family

Flowers: Two-tone yellow flowers with two lips in a dense column. Upper lip has two lobes and faces upward. Lower lip has three lobes and an orange patch. A trailing spur projects back and downwards.

Leaves: Narrow, gray-green, numerous.

Size: 1-3 ft; flowers ¾-1 inch long.

Season: June to September

Habitat: Plains to Montane
Disturbed areas, such as roadsides.

Notes: This appealing wild snapdragon, and its larger relative, Dalmatian Toadflax (*L. genistifolia dalmatica*), are troublesome aggressive weeds.

OWL CLOVER

Orthocarpus luteus
Figwort family

Flowers: Tiny, yellow, two-lipped flowers scattered among green leaf-like bracts, along a vertical spike.

Leaves: Narrow, alternate and short.

Size: 4-12 inches; flowers ¼ inch long.

Season: July through September

Habitat: Foothills and Montane Common in open dry areas.

Notes: This plant is not a clover and has nothing to do with owls.

BRACTED LOUSEWORT

Pedicularis bracteosa paysoniana
Figwort family

Flowers: Yellow, narrow tubular flowers in a dense column. Flowers have two tiny lips and curve downward near the tips.

Leaves: Finely divided, fern-like leaves, alternate along the stem.

Size: 1-3 ft; flowers ¾-1 inch long.

Season: June to August

Habitat: Montane and Subalpine
Grows in moist meadows and wooded areas.

YELLOW MONKEYFLOWER

Mimulus guttatus
Figwort family

Flowers: Bright yellow, tubular flowers with a two-lobed upper lip and three-lobed lower lip. There are two humps on the lower lip which nearly close the throat and are covered with yellow hairs and a few red dots.

Leaves: Opposite, oval, with toothed edges.

Size: 1-3 ft; flowers ½-1½ inches long.

Season: May to September

Habitat: Foothills to Subalpine
Grows in very wet areas, along streams, seeps, ditches and ponds.

Notes: The shape of the flower is supposed to resemble a laughing monkey.

NORTHERN PAINTBRUSH
SULPHUR PAINTBRUSH

Castilleja sulphurea
Figwort family

Flowers: A dense cluster of pale yellow bracts obscures the actual flowers, which are very thin, green and tubular, each with a bump at its tip.

Leaves: Alternate, lance-shaped, smooth.

Size: 6-20 inches; flowers ¾-1 inch long.

Season: June to August

Habitat: Foothills to Subalpine
Grows in moist meadows, hillsides and forest clearings.

Notes: A very similar yellow paintbrush of higher elevations is the Western Paintbrush *(Castilleja occidentalis)*.

115

GOLDEN SMOKE

Corydalis aurea
Fumitory family

Flowers: Loose clusters of tubular yellow flowers on a bushy plant. The upper petal forms a curved hood in front and a long spur behind. The lower petal hangs down, and two side petals join to enclose the stamens.

Leaves: Twice divided into thin soft segments.

Size: 4-16 inches; flowers ½-¾ inch long.

Season: May to September

Habitat: Plains to Montane
Prefers dry gravelly areas, open woods and disturbed areas.

GLACIER LILY
AVALANCHE LILY

Erythronium grandiflorum
Lily family

Flowers: Spectacular large yellow flowers with six curled tepals and protruding stamens.

Leaves: Two long, lance-shaped, basal leaves.

Size: 6-12 inches; flowers 2-3 inches wide.

Season: May to August

Habitat: Montane to Alpine
Found in moist meadows and open woods, often near retreating snowbanks in late spring.

Notes: The term "tepals" refers to both petals and sepals when they are indistinguishable. Other common names for this flower are Fawn Lily, Snow Lily, and Dogtooth Violet.

WESTERN WALLFLOWER

Erysimum capitatum
Mustard family

Flowers: A tight round cluster of small yellow or orange flowers, each with four petals.

Leaves: Long and narrow, sometimes slightly toothed.

Size: 8-24 inches; flowers ½-1 inch wide.

Season: May to July

Habitat: Plains to Montane
Common in open meadows, hills and plains.

GOLDEN BANNER
GOLDEN PEA

Thermopsis divaricarpa
Pea family

Flowers: Loose clusters of bright yellow pea-type flowers.

Leaves: Palmately compound with three leaflets.

Size: 1-3 ft; flowers ¾-1 inch long.

Season: April to July

Habitat: Foothills to Subalpine Abundant in open and gravelly areas, meadows and roadsides.

ALPINE AVENS

Acomastylis rossii turbinata
Rose family

Flowers: Bright yellow flowers with five rounded petals and five pointed green sepals.

Leaves: Finely dissected, fern-like leaves in a dense cushion.

Size: 3-10 inches; flowers ¾ inch wide.

Season: Late June to August

Habitat: Alpine
Abundant on open tundra, often forming huge areas of yellow.

Notes: The leaves turn deep red in autumn.

SHRUBBY CINQUEFOIL

Pentaphylloides floribunda
Rose family

Flowers: Many bright yellow flowers, each with five round petals.

Leaves: Narrow leaflets, pinnately compound, greyish-green on a bushy shrub.

Size: 1-3 ft; flowers ¾-1½ inches wide.

Season: June to September

Habitat: Foothills to Alpine
Common in many areas, clearings, meadows and woods.

Notes: This plant is also called 'Potentilla' and often used as an ornamental shrub.

YELLOW STONECROP

Amerosedum lanceolatum
Stonecrop family

Flowers: Small yellow flowers with five yellow pointed petals and ten stamens, at the top of a fleshy erect stem.

Leaves: Alternate, succulent, grayish-green and banana-shaped.

Size: 3-8 inches; flowers ¼ inch wide.

Season: June to August

Habitat: Plains to Alpine
Very common in sunny, dry, rocky areas.

122

YELLOW POND LILY

Nuphar luteum polysepala
Water Lily family

Flowers: Large spherical, bright yellow flowers, held slightly above the water's surface.

Leaves: Very large, heart-shaped leaves which lay on the surface of the water.

Size: 1-2 ft; flowers 3-5 inches wide.

Season: July and August

Habitat: Montane and Subalpine
Grows in shallow areas of ponds and lakes.

Index of Latin Names

Index of Common Names